Love

Poems *Nikki*

Giovanni

William Morrow and Company, Inc. *New York*

Library of Congress Cataloging-in-Publication Data

Giovanni, Nikki.
Love poems / Nikki Giovanni.
p. cm.
ISBN 0-688-14989-8
1. Love poetry, American. 2. Afro-Americans—Poetry. I. Title.
PS3557.I55L68 1997
811'.54—dc2096-43698
CIP

Printed in the United States of America

First Edition

3 4 5 6 7 8 9 10

BOOK DESIGN BY LEAH S. CARLSON

FOR TUPAC SHAKUR (1971–1996)

a lover whose love was often deliberately misunderstood
but who will live in the sun and the rains and whose name
will echo through all the winds whose spirit will flower and
who like Emmett Till and Malcolm X will be remembered
by his people for the great man he could have become and
most especially for the beautiful boy that he was

CONTENTS

I. *I Hope It's Love*   11

What It Is   13
That Day   15
The Way I Feel   17
Kidnap Poem   19
Giddiyap   20
I Wrote a Good Omelet   22
A Summer Love Poem   23
Communication   24
Love Is   25
I Do Have My Likes and Dislikes   26
Seduction   27
Things That Go Together   28
And I Have You   29
A Poem of Friendship   30
My House   31
Just a Simple Declaration of Love   33
Beautiful Black Men   34
You Were Gone   36
Cancers   37
The Only True Lovers Are Chefs or Happy Birthday,
Edna Lewis   39

II. *And Yeah . . . These Are Love Poems*   43

A Greater Love of God and Country   44
For Tommy   46
Mothers   47
A Poem *for langston hughes*   49

When Gamble and Huff Ruled 50

You Are There 53

And Yeah . . . This Is A Love Poem 55

Swaziland 59

For Theresa 60

All Eyez On U 62

III. *I Take Master Card (Charge Your Love to Me)* 65

A Theory of Pole Beans 67

No Furnaces (For Valentine's Day) 69

August 70

Poetry Is a Trestle 71

1995 73

A Happy Reason 74

Balances 75

Love In Place 76

Three/Quarters Time 77

Resignation 78

Poem 81

Luxury 82

When I Nap 83

The Butterfly 84

I Want To Sing 85

Rain 86

How Do You Write a Poem? 87

Just a New York Poem 89

Telephone Poem 91

You Came, Too 92

Her Flying Trapeze 93

I Take Master Card 94

In All Seasons 96

Love
Poems

I

I   H o p e   I t ' s   L o v e

What It Is

if it's a trail we can hike it
if it has two wheels we can bike it

if it's an allergy we can sneeze it
if it's a pimple we can squeeze it

if it's dew it "covers Dixie"
if it's Tinker Bell it's a pixie

if it's a breeze it can blow us
if it's the sun it can know us

if it's a song we can sing it
if it flies we can wing it

if it's soda pop then it's drinkable
it might be X-Rated but that's unthinkable

if it's a boat we can sail it
if it's a letter we can mail it

if it's a star we can let it shine
if it's the moon it can make you mine

if it's grass we can rake it
if it's free why not take it

if it's a tide it can ebb
if it's a spider it can web

if it's chocolate we can dip it
if it's a golf ball we can chip it

if it's gum we can chew it
I hope it's love so we can do it

That Day

if you've got the key
then i've got the door
let's do what we did
when we did it before

if you've got the time
i've got the way
let's do what we did
when we did it all day

you get the glass
i've got the wine
we'll do what we did
when we did it overtime

if you've got the dough
then i've got the heat
we can use my oven
til it's warm and sweet

i know i'm bold
coming on like this
but the good things in life
are too good to be missed

now time is money
and money is sweet
if you're busy baby
we can do it on our feet

we can do it on the floor
we can do it on the stair
we can do it on the couch
we can do it in the air

we can do it in the grass
and in case we get an itch
i can scratch it with my left hand
cause i'm really quite a witch

if we do it once a month
we can do it in time
if we do it once a week
we can do it in rhyme
if we do it every day
we can do it everyway
we can do it like we did it
when we did it
that day

The Way I Feel

i've noticed i'm happier
when i make love
with you
and have enough left
over to smile at my doorman

i've realized i'm fulfilled
like a big fat cow
who was just picked
for a carnation contentment
when you kiss your special place
right behind my knee

i'm as glad as mortar
on a brick that knows
another brick is coming
when you walk through
my door

most time when you're around
i feel like a note
roberta flack is going to sing

in my mind you're a clock
and i'm the second hand sweeping
around you sixty times an hour
twenty-four hours a day

three hundred sixty-five days a year
and an extra day
in leap year
cause that's the way
that's the way
that's the way i feel
about you

Kidnap Poem

ever been kidnapped
by a poet
if i were a poet
i'd kidnap you
put you in my phrases and meter
you to jones beach
or maybe coney island
or maybe just to my house
lyric you in lilacs
dash you in the rain
blend into the beach
to complement my see
play the lyre for you
ode you with my love song
anything to win you
wrap you in the red Black green
show you off to mama
yeah if i were a poet i'd kid
nap you

Giddiyap

my old man is as fat as he can be
my old man is as wide as the deep blue sea
what i do for him he does for me

we don't fly and rarely take a train
mostly we enjoy our own terrain
sitting on a rocker in the rain

singing

giddiyap horsie giddiyap
giddi giddi giddi giddi giddiyap
giddiyap horsie giddiyap
giddi giddi giddi giddiyap
riding on the top of a silver lined cloud singing giddiyap out loud

my old man says he would lose for me
get as slim as i would want to see
but all that him is him enough for me

i'm not lazy neither am i shy
i don't worry neither do i cry
when he touches me i want to die

shouting

giddiyap horsie giddiyap
giddi giddi giddi giddi giddiyap
riding on a rainbow cloud singing shouting giddiyap out loud

I Wrote a Good Omelet

I wrote a good omelet . . . and ate a hot poem . . .
after loving you

Buttoned my car . . . and drove my coat home . . . in the
rain . . .
after loving you

I goed on red . . . and stopped on green . . . floating
somewhere in between . . .
being here and being there . . .
after loving you

I rolled my bed . . . turned down my hair . . . slightly
confused but . . . I don't care . . .
Laid out my teeth . . . and gargled my gown . . . then I stood
. . . and laid me down . . .
to sleep . . .
after loving you

A Summer Love Poem

clouds float by on a summer sky   i hop scotch over to you

rainbows arch from ground to gold   i climb over to you

thunder grumbles   lightning tumbles and i bounce over to you

sun beams back and catches me   smiling over at you

Communication

if music is the most universal language
just think of me as one whole note

if science has the most perfect language
picture me as MC^2

since mathematics can speak to the infinite
imagine me as 1 to the first power

what i mean is   one day
i'm gonna grab your love
and you'll be
satisfied

Seduction

one day
you gonna walk in this house
and i'm gonna have on a long African
gown
you'll sit down and say "The Black . . ."
and i'm gonna take one arm out
then you—not noticing me at all—will say "What about
this brother . . ."
and i'm going to be slipping it over my head
and you'll rap on about "The revolution . . ."
while i rest your hand against my stomach
you'll go on—as you always do—saying
"I just can't dig . . ."
while i'm moving your hand up and down
and i'll be taking your dashiki off
then you'll say "What we really need . . ."
and i'll be licking your arm
and "The way I see it we ought to . . ."
and unbuckling your pants
"And what about the situation . . ."
and taking your shorts off
then you'll notice
your state of undress
and knowing you you'll just say
"Nikki,
isn't this counterrevolutionary . . . ?"

Things That Go Together

Let's start with the air which has its airplanes
And thunder
And lightning
And kites

Then think of the bulbs which have shades
And switches
To turn on
When we need night lights

Oysters have seas   Some dogs have fleas
though bricks and mortar are sticking

Rock has its roll   Bay Bridge: No Toll
and pillows have cases and ticking

And tumbling through Space with a smile on its face
The moon has its wine and its cheeses

The Jeopardy answer is: You and Me
The question is: Who likes squeezes

And I Have You

Rain has drops   Sun has shine
Moon has beams   That make you mine

Rivers have banks   Sands for shores
Hearts have heartbeats   That make me yours

Needles have eyes   Though pins may prick
Elmer has glue   To make things stick

Winter has Spring   Stockings feet
Pepper has mint   To make it sweet

Teachers have lessons   Soup du jour
Lawyers sue bad folks   Doctors cure

All and all this much is true
You have me   And I have you

A Poem of Friendship

We are not lovers
because of the love
we make
but the love
we have

We are not friends
because of the laughs
we spend
but the tears
we save

I don't want to be near you
for the thoughts we share
but the words we never have
to speak

I will never miss you
because of what we do
but what we are
together

My House

i only want to
be there to kiss you
as you want to be kissed
when you need to be kissed
where i want to kiss you
cause it's my house
and i plan to live in it

i really need to hug you
when i want to hug you
as you like to hug me
does this sound like a silly poem

i mean it's my house
and i want to fry pork chops
and bake sweet potatoes
and call them yams
cause i run the kitchen
and i can stand the heat

i spent all winter in
carpet stores gathering
patches so i could make
a quilt
does this really sound
like a silly poem
i mean i want to keep you
warm

and my windows might be dirty
but it's my house
and if i can't see out sometimes
they can't see in either

english isn't a good language
to express emotion through
mostly i imagine because people
try to speak english instead
of trying to speak through it
i don't know maybe it is
a silly poem

i'm saying it's my house
and i'll make fudge and call
it love and touch my lips
to the chocolate warmth
and smile at old men and call
that revolution cause what's real
is really real
and i still like men in tight
pants cause everybody has some
thing to give and more
important needs something to take

and this is my house and you make me
happy
so this is your poem

Just a Simple Declaration of Love

In the reddish gray of morning just before night concedes I know the
silhouette of Sunflowers turning their heads to the east

I hear birds gathering at the bird bath chattering away   singing
warning   gossiping about the cat in the bushes

I watch the rabbits starting for the warren under my shed to rest
from another night of survival

Mother 'Possum with six youngsters on her back slowly like any
other overburdened woman makes her way back home

I look at the clouds push off against the lighter blue
                                    and
making coffee I hear the friendly gurgle of the drip maker
the sigh of the toast softly browning

I watch my world come awake sitting in my kitchen hearing smelling
tasting another day but nothing is clear until you

Smile

Calling the sun to work

Beautiful Black Men

(With compliments and apologies to all not mentioned by name)

i wanta say just gotta say something
bout those beautiful beautiful beautiful outasight
black men
with they afros
walking down the street
is the same ol danger
but a brand new pleasure

sitting on stoops, in bars, going to offices
running numbers, watching for their whores
preaching in churches, driving their hogs
walking their dogs, winking at me
in their fire red, lime green, burnt orange
royal blue tight tight pants that hug
what i like to hug

jerry butler, wilson pickett, the impressions
temptations, mighty mighty sly
don't have to do anything but walk
on stage
and i scream and stamp and shout
see new breed men in breed alls
dashiki suits with shirts that match
the lining that complements the ties

that smile at the sandals
where dirty toes peek at me
and i scream and stamp and shout
for more beautiful beautiful beautiful
black men with outasight afros

You Were Gone

You were gone
like a fly lighting
on that wall
with a spider in the corner

You were gone
like last week's paycheck
for this week's bills

You were gone
like the years between
twenty-five and thirty
as if somehow

You never existed
and if it wouldn't be
for the gray hairs
I'd never know that

You had come

Cancers

(not necessarily a love poem)

Cancers are a serious condition . . . attacking internal organs
 . . . eating
them away . . . or clumping lumps . . . together . . .

The blood vessels carry . . . cancerous cells . . . to all body
parts . . . cruising
would be the term . . . but this is not necessarily a love
poem . . .

Cancer is caused . . . by . . .
the air we breathe
the food we eat
the water we drink
Indices are unusually high . . . in cities that have baseball
teams
 . . . or people . . .

Coffee . . . milk . . . saccharine
cigarettes . . . sun . . . and birth control
devices . . .
are among the chief offenders . . .
Monthly phenomena stopped . . . internally . . . will
only lead . . .
to shock syndrome . . .
What indeed . . . porcelana . . . does a woman . . . want . . .

Cancers are . . .
the new plague
the modern black death
all that is unknown
yet

I have a cancer . . . in my heart . . . I'm told . . . on
knowledgeable authority . . .
it is not possible
For the heart we have . . .
cardiac arrest . . . and outright attacks . . .
holes in valves . . . and valve stoppage . . .
constricted vessels . . . and nefarious air
bubbles . . .

But then . . . my doctor never saw you . . . and doesn't
believe
  . . . in the zodiac . . .

The Only True Lovers Are Chefs or Happy Birthday, Edna Lewis

it is practically amazing///a show of immense proportions. . . more awe inspiring . . . more death defying . . . more dangerous than hanging from some very thin rope at the top of the very big tent . . . more difficult than putting the lions and tigers in the same cage . . . more better than anything at all///that mothers cook meals each day for ungrateful children and spouses

if we were fair about it///we would enclose all kitchens in glass . . . so that the passers by would stop and wonder at the Ralston's bubbling in the Pyrex double boiler each morning and the beauty of the four plates stacked against the four glasses tucking the forks and knives with that wonderful gentle touch of a napkin just kissing the edge///if we were really fair we would hold contests for the ordinary housewife who is not an ordinary anything but a working mother though we recognize immediately that there is no concept of a working father though we all are told men have families too so that we might reward the best housewife with some sort of Silver Plate and the best housemother with a Silver Child and the best working housewifemother with a Silver Husband studded with rubies and sapphires and one $1/4$ carat diamond///if we were fair about it

but this is about love and there can be no better loving than bread pudding oh sure I know some people who think bread pudding is just food but some people also think creamed corn comes in a can and they have never known the pure ecstasy of slicing down the thicker end of an ear of silver queen that was just picked at five or six this very same morning then having sliced it down so very neatly you take the back of the knife and pull it all back up releasing that wonderful milk to the bowl to which you add a pinch of garlic and some fresh ground pepper which you then turn into a gently lit skillet and you shimmer it all like eggs then put a piece of aluminum foil over it and let it rest while you put your hands at the small of your back and go "Whew" and ain't that love that soaks cold chicken wings in buttermilk and gets the heavy iron pot out and puts just the right pat of lard in it at a high temperature so that when you dust the wings with a little seasoned flour the lard sizzles and cracks while the wings turn all golden on the outside and juicy on the inside and yes I'd say that's love all right cause that other stuff anybody can do and if you do it long enough you can do it either well or adequately but cooking///now that is something you learn from your heart then make your hands do what your grandmother's hands did and I still don't trust anyone who makes meatloaf with instruments cause the meat is to be turned with your hands and while this may not be a traditional love poem let me just say one small thing for castor oil and Vicks VapoRub and "How is my little baby feeling today?" after a hard day's work so yes this is a love poem of the highest order because the next best cook in the world, my grandmother being the best, just had a birthday and all the asparagus and wild greens and quail and tomatoes on the vines and little peas in spring and half runners in early summer and all the wonderful musty things that come from the ground said EDNA LEWIS is having a birthday and all of us who love all of you who love food wish her a happy birthday because we who are really smart know that chefs make the best lovers .... especially when they serve it with oysters on the half shell

II

And Yeah . . . These Are Love Poems

A Greater Love of God and Country

Concerning the Burning of Old and Alone Though Not Lonely
Black Churches

There is no reason to ask
"WHY" since to ask "WHY" is to enter some dark and crazy spot
where one presumes there is REASON and A REASON that will
make sense which is not to say there is a craziness: I don't believe
this is crazy but rather mean . . . hateful . . . ugly—though not igno-
rant because there is knowledge here and there is a purpose here
but there is NO
REASON

People who will burn a cross will burn a church

The buildings may be rebuilt but the creak
of a stair . . . the smell of the polish in the pews
the old kitchen where Sunday dinners were reheated
the icebox where the iced tea was kept . . . the too narrow
steps leading to the damp and dusky basement . . . the leaky
window that could not always keep the cold at bay . . . the knowing
that this building was built by these hands to worship this God who
has Delivered us . . . . No . . . that cannot be rebuilt

The people who have burned crosses will burn a church

Something will be lost and the world just a bit sadder
for the loss of the building. . . . But the people who sift through
ashes know that fire is a friend and that fire can be a foe
But the people who use fire are lowdown . . .
And the people who know that some people are lowdown will watch
the fires . . . will forgive the trespasses . . . and will go right on
thanking their God for His powerful . . . magnificent

Deliverance

For Tommy

to tommy who:
eats chocolate cookies and lamb chops
climbs stairs and cries when i change his diaper
lets me hold him only on his schedule
defined my nature
and gave me a new name (mommy)
which supersedes all others
controls my life
and makes me glad
that he does

Mothers

the last time i was home
to see my mother we kissed
exchanged pleasantries
and unpleasantries pulled a warm
comforting silence around
us and read separate books

i remember the first time
i consciously saw her
we were living in a three room
apartment on burns avenue

mommy always sat in the dark
i don't know how i knew that but she did

that night i stumbled into the kitchen
maybe because i've always been
a night person or perhaps because i had wet
the bed
she was sitting on a chair
the room was bathed in moonlight diffused through
    tiny window panes
she may have been smoking but maybe not
her hair was three-quarters her height
which made me a strong believer in the samson myth
and very black

i'm sure i just hung there by the door
i remember thinking: what a beautiful lady
she was very deliberately waiting
perhaps for my father to come home
from his night job or maybe for a dream
that had promised to come by
"come here" she said "i'll teach you
a poem: *i see the moon*

>*the moon sees me*
>*god bless the moon*
>*and god bless me"*

i taught that to my son
who recited it for her
just to say we must learn
to bear the pleasures
as we have borne the pains

that's when the music was for us about us by us and gamble and huff didn't take a gamble or huff but righteously brought the music out of us to place it back in us and, hey, they want to talk about Intruders and i always loved those brothers 'cause that's what we all are if other people have their way i mean. . . . Intruders?

that's when in some wild and wonderful way we were courageous enough to still fall in love and crazy enough not to hold back and sensible enough not to cry when it was over nor whine nor beg and plead and threaten but just find another love for another day and even if people thought we were trite and silly we knew we were just expressing a brand new us and oh you had better believe the people were ready for that train a coming

that's when we were strong and determined to change the world and if not change it leave it different from when we first met it and i like black people for that

i like us for our faith and our energy and loving our mamas and ourselves and the world and all the chances we took in trying to make everything better which we did for some and definitely not for others and i dislike other people for taking our music our muse and our rap to sell their cars and bread and toothpaste and deodorant and sneakers but never seeming to have enough to give back to the people who created it and that's not a huff or a gamble but the awful truth of white america that's when the possibility was possible and we got in our orange beetles and drove across country and back and rocked and rolled into a newer possibility while lassoing and harnessing and ultimately riding the night winds that bucked and resisted but we held on and we were right and the possibilities closed down but the beat goes on the beat goes on the beat beat beat goes right on

that's when

You Are There

i shall save my poems
for the winter of my dreams
i look forward to huddling
in my rocker with my life
i wonder what i'll contemplate
lovers—certainly those
i can remember
and knowing my life
you'll be there

you'll be there in the cold
like a Siamese on my knee
proud purring when you let me stroke you

you'll be there in the rain
like an umbrella over my head
sheltering me from the damp mist

you'll be there in the dark
like a lighthouse in the fog
seeing me through troubled waters

you'll be there in the sun
like coconut oil on my back
to keep me from burning

i shall save a special poem
for you to say
you always made me smile
and even though i cried sometimes
you said i will not let you
down

my rocker and i on winter's porch
will never be sad if you're gone
the winter's cold has been stored
against
you will always be
there

And Yeah . . . This Is A Love Poem
(October 16, 1995)

It's not that I don't respect the brother in Baltimore or Washington
or even some parts of Northern Virginia because I do   It's just that
this is different

The brother who had to wake up before dawn, get into a car that may
or may not need a new muffler, a new set of spark plugs, some atten-
tion to the motor but who decided none the less that "Yes" he had
to heed the call to go to Washington DC   That's the brother I want
to talk about

Not at all, please understand,   that I don't have a high regard for
the brother who got on the bus   Getting on buses has always been
a central revolutionary act of Black America   Just ask Plessy or
Parks No   Getting on a bus is an act of responsibility   An act of
bravery
An act of commitment to change

But the brother who rose from his warm bed   Who made his own
coffee because his wife pretended to be asleep because she was
scared that he might not come back alive and she didn't want to let
him see her fear in her eyes 'cause she knew he needed to go even
if he wouldn't come back alive   That's the brother I want to talk
about here

I want to talk about the young brother who just didn't understand why everything he did no matter how hard he tried never seemed to come out right How if he went bowling and got nine pins the 10th pin would just stand there mocking the ball heading for the gutter How if he bumped into someone on the street and said a simple "I'm sorry" somebody else would jump in his face but if he didn't say anything then someone said he was uncouth or how sometimes people would even deliberately run into him so he joined with other people like him and instead of calling it a Benevolent Society or a Brotherhood or something wonderful and romantic like Elks and Masons and Lions or Rotarians they called it a "Gang" indicating it was a "nest" of "vipers" and terms like that indicating things that we find dirty and unacceptable How when four or five white boys rape a mentally handicapped girl they are just exercising bad judgment but when four or five black boys rape a jogger they are all animals and this is not for any brother who rapes any female and it's not for anyone who hurts women or other vulnerable life forms but just a word or two about black boys who don't understand why everything they ever tried to do just never seems to turn out right and I think "Of course" "Yes" "Why wouldn't they cry themselves to sleep" when all that they want and want to be they already know is denied them Why wouldn't they be afraid of the dark Why wouldn't their hearts be broken when the people they love . . . mothers . . . fathers . . . aunts . . . uncles . . . girlfriends . . . good buddies . . . teachers . . . preachers . . . all turn out to be untrue And please don't tell me that basketball and baseball and football aren't the way to go that they should get their education when their education will only tell them to get a talent because the people who get up if not out of these cesspools we call the inner city have something more than a high school degree behind them and you have to be some kind of real fool to not see that they see who makes the money and who doesn't This is for the brother, however, who does, indeed, believe that there can be   should be   must be   a change

It's not that I am in any way unhappy about the brother who has a fine home, a car that is always serviced on time, a job with health benefits, a pretty wife, happy smart children, a dog that obeys. I'm proud and happy for him and his because I know a people cannot do better unless individuals do better but this is about the brother who stands on the street corners singing five part a cappela harmony and the brother who does break dancing under the street lights and the brothers who created rap because they took the music classes away so the brothers scratched then they invented CDs so the brothers rapped then they said Rap is the enemy of women as if Bob Dole and Rush Limbaugh and self satisfied Republicans with bumper sticker mentalities don't exist so this is for the brother who is simply trying to find a tone to soothe his soul while everyone wants to make him the reason America is way off track

And this is about the brother who knowing he is a better person than even he thinks he is got in his car in Detroit or Cincinnati or St. Louis and headed for Washington not knowing if he would be the only brother to show up for the Day of Atonement but knowing if he was the only brother then on this day at this time he would be the brother to stand and say to himself, his brothers and the folks whom he loves and who love him I Am Sorry That Things Are Not Different and that is a mighty powerful thing to say because people want to make you make miracles when all any of us can actually say is I Wish It Would Be Different but this is for the brother who was willing to be the only brother so that if there would be laughter as he stood alone on the Mall he still said I will stand because today it doesn't matter if I am alone I need to stand and testify and yeah this is a love poem for that brother who decided for this one point in time I will be my better self . . . And we all are very proud of you

Swaziland

i am old and need
to remember
you are young and need
to learn
if i forget the words
will you remember the music

i hear a drum speaking of a stream
the path is crossing the stream
the stream is crossing the path
which came first the drums ask
the music is with the river

if we meet does it matter
that i took the step toward you

the words ask are you fertile
the music says let's dance

i am old and need to remember
you are young and want to learn
let's dance together
let's dance
together
let's
dance
together

For Theresa

and when i was all alone
facing my adolescence
looking forward
to cleaning house
and reading books
and maybe learning bridge
so that i could fit
into acceptable society
acceptably
you came along
and loved me
for being black and bitchy
hateful and scared
and you came along
and cared that i got
all the things necessary
to adulthood
and even made sure
i wouldn't hate
my mother
or father
and you even understood
that i should love
peppe
but not too much
and give to gary
but not all of me

and keep on moving
'til i found me
and now you're sick
and have been hurt
for some time
and i've felt guilty
and impotent
for not being able
to give yourself
to you
as you gave
yourself
to me

All Eyez On U

(for 2Pac Shakur 1971–1996)

as I tossed and turned unable to achieve sleep unable to control
anxiety unable to comprehend why

2Pac is not with us

if those who lived by the sword died by the sword there would be no
white men on earth
if those who lived on hatred died on hatred there would be no KKK
if those who lived by lies died by lies there would be nobody on wall
street in executive suites in academic offices instructing the young
don't tell me he got what he deserved   he deserved a chariot and
the accolades of a grateful people

he deserved his life

it is as clear as a mountain stream as defining as a lightning strike
as terrifying as sun to vampires

2Pac told the truth

there were those who called it dirty   gansta rap inciting there were
those who never wanted to be   angry at the conditions but angry
at the messenger who reported: *your kitchen has roaches your toi-
let is overflowing your basement has so much water the rats are in the
living room*
<u>*your house is in disorder*</u>

and 2Pac told you about it

what a beautiful boy graceful carriage melodic voice sharp wit intel-
lectual breadth what a beautiful boy to lose

not me   never me   I do not believe east coast west coast   I saw
them murder Emmett Till I saw them murder Malcolm X   I saw
them murder   Martin Luther King   I witnessed them shooting
Rap Brown I saw them beat LeRoi Jones   I saw them fill their jails
I see them burning churches   not me   never me   I do not believe
this is some sort of mouth action   this is some sort of political
action and they picked well   they picked the brightest freshest
fruit from the tallest tree   what a beautiful boy

but he will not go away   as Malcolm did not go away   as Emmett
Till did not go away   your shooting him will not take him from us
his spirit will fill our hearts   his courage will strengthen us for the
challenge   his truth will straighten our backbones

you know, Socrates had a mother   she too watched her son drink
hemlock   she too asked why   but Socrates stood firm and would
not lie to save himself   2Pac has a mother   the lovely Afeni had
to bury her son   it is not right

it is not right that this young warrior is cut down   it is not right for
the old to bury the young   it is not right

this generation mourns 2Pac as my generation mourned Till as we
all mourn Malcolm   this wonderful young warrior

Sonia Sanchez said when she learned of his passing she walked all day walking the beautiful warrior home to our ancestors I just cried as all mothers cry for the beautiful boy who said he and Mike Tyson would never be allowed to be free at the same time who told the truth about them and who told the truth about us who is our beautiful warrior

there are those who wanted to make *him* the problem   who wanted to believe if they silenced 2Pac all would be quiet on the ghetto front there are those who testified that the problem wasn't the conditions but the people talking about them

they took away band   so the boys started scratching they took away gym   so the boys started break dancing the boys started rapping cause they gave them the guns and the drugs but not the schools and libraries

what a beautiful boy to lose

and we mourn 2Pac Shakur and we reach out to his mother and we hug ourselves in sadness and shame

and we are compelled to ask:
R U Happy, Mz Tucker? 2Pac is gone
R U Happy?

III

I Take Master Card
(Charge Your Love
to Me)

A Theory of Pole Beans

(for Ethel and Rice)

that must have been the tail end of the Depression
as well as the depression of coming war
there certainly was segregation and hatred and fear

these small towns and small minded people
trying to bend taller spirits down
were unable to succeed

there couldn't have been too much fun
assuming fun equates with irresponsibility

there was always food to be put on the table
clothes to be washed and ironed
hair to be pressed
gardens to be weeded

and children to talk to and teach
each other to love
and tend to

pole beans are not everyone's favorite
they make you think of pieces of fat back
cornbread
and maybe a piece of fried chicken

they are the staples of things unquestioned
they are broken and boiled

no one would say life handed you
a silver spoon or golden parachute
but you still
met   married
bought a home   reared a family
supported a church   and kept a mighty faith
in your God   and each other

they say love/is a many splendored thing
but maybe that's because we recognize
you loved no matter what the burden
you laughed no matter for the tears
you persevered in your love

and your garden remains in full bloom

No Furnaces (For Valentine's Day)

I don't understand why   my hands   are cold . . . What am I try-
ing to prove . . .   That I can keep the house as cold . . . as you do
. . .   even when you're not here . . . That my feet and hands don't
care . . . I think not . . . I think it's a simple desire . . . unstated even
to myself . . . to acknowledge . . . that when you're not here . . . it's
always cold . . . and the furnace . . . can   not . . . possibly . . . make
a   difference

August

Apples fall   peaches harvested
One kind of pear is prickled

Blackberries turn your fingers blue
Some cucumbers get pickled

Biscuits bake or they are fried
Grits are cooked real slow

Green tomatoes in bacon fat
Then it's time to go

From Grandmother's country home
Back up to the city

I'd rather stay in the barefoot South
where everything is pretty

Poetry Is a Trestle

poetry is a trestle
spanning the distance between
what i feel
and what i say

like a locomotive
i rush full speed ahead
trusting your strength
to carry me over

sometimes we share a poem
because people are near
and they would notice me
noticing you
so i write X and you write O
and we both win

sometimes we share a poem
because i'm washing the dishes
and you're looking at your news

or sometimes we make a poem
because it's Sunday and you want
ice cream while i want cookies

but always we share a poem
because belief predates action
and i believe
the most beautiful poem
ever heard is your heart
racing

1995

it was an unusual weather season///there had been thunderstorms in the winter/snow in June///volcanoes exploding all over the place/// tropical waves from the western shore of Africa ///floods in Indiana and Texas in drought///planes fell and boats sunk///arch deluxe was not a hit and nobody drank diet Pepsi///it was going to be a longlong season but somehow during the hailstorm just before the tornado we met///and the tulip tree blossomed and the river birch sighed///the day lilies flowered///the butterflies flittered by///lightning bugs sang///and you and I wished on the new moon///and though we only had one number of the Pennsylvania lottery we were winners in that wild and crazy year///when everything turned upside down and all around///and we all lived in "a musical go thing" with the snow ///and the ice skating boy///inside

A Happy Reason

a good book (not necessarily a mystery) . . . some popcorn with lots of
real butter . . . an overstuffed chair . . . a fire in the wood stove . . .
quilts on the couch . . . thermal blankets on the bed . . . a feather
duster waiting to be used . . . a merlot waiting to be explored . . . the
coffee pot with a timer . . . the 49ers winning if we get lucky . . . comic
pages in color . . . intelligent editorials . . . snow or rain or any
inclement weather . . . or heavy doses of sun . . . a reason to move or
not move . . . a reason to go   or not go   no reason to be
anything . . .
except happy . . .
with . . .
you

Balances

in life
one is always
balancing

like we juggle our mothers
against our fathers

or one teacher
against another
(only to balance our grade average)

3 grains salt
to one ounce truth

our sweet black essence
or the funky honkies down the street

and lately i've begun wondering
if you're trying to tell me something

we used to talk all night
and do things alone together

and i've begun
(as a reaction to a feeling)
to balance
the pleasure of loneliness
against the pain
of loving you

Love In Place

I really don't remember falling in love all that much
I remember wanting to bake corn bread and boil a ham and I
certainly remember making lemon pie and when I used to smoke I
stopped in the middle of my day to contemplate

I know I must have fallen in love once because I quit biting
my cuticles and my hair is gray and that must indicate
something and I all of a sudden had a deeper appreciation
for Billie Holiday and Billy Strayhorn so if it wasn't love I don't
know what it was

I see the old photographs and I am smiling and I'm sure quite
happy but what I mostly see is me
through your eyes
and I am still young and slim and very much committed to the
love we still have

Three/Quarters Time

Dance with me . . . dance with me . . . we are the song . . . we
are the music . . .
Dance with me . . .

Waltz me . . . twirl me . . . do-si-do please . . . peppermint
twist me . . . philly
Squeeze

Cha cha cha . . . tango . . . two step too . . .
Cakewalk . . . charleston . . . bougaloo . . .

Dance with me . . . dance with me . . . all night long . . .
We are the music . . . we are the song . . .

Resignation

I love you
because the Earth turns round the sun
because the North wind blows north
sometimes
because the Pope is Catholic
and most Rabbis Jewish
because winters flow into springs
and the air clears after a storm
because only my love for you
despite the charms of gravity
keeps me from falling off this Earth
into another dimension
I love you
because it is the natural order of things

I love you
like the habit I picked up in college
of sleeping through lectures
{ or saying I'm sorry
{ when I get stopped for speeding
because I drink a glass of water
in the morning
and chain-smoke cigarettes
all through the day
because I take my coffee Black
and my milk with chocolate
because you keep my feet warm

78

though my life a mess
I love you
because I don't want it
any other way

I am helpless
in my love for you
It makes me so happy
to hear you call my name
I am amazed you can resist
locking me in an echo chamber
where your voice reverberates
through the four walls
sending me into spasmatic ecstasy
I love you
because it's been so good
for so long
that if I didn't love you
I'd have to be born again
and that is not a theological statement
I am pitiful in my love for you

The Dells tell me Love
is so simple
the thought though of you
sends indescribably delicious multitudenous
thrills throughout and through-in my body
I love you
because no two snowflakes are alike

and it is possible
if you stand tippy-toe
to walk between the raindrops
I love you
because I am afraid of the dark
and can't sleep in the light
because I rub my eyes
when I wake up in the morning
and find you there
because you with all your magic powers were
determined that
I should love you
because there was nothing for you but that
I would love you
I love you
because you made me
want to love you
more than I love my privacy
my freedom my commitments
and responsibilities
I love you 'cause I changed my life
to love you
because you saw me one friday
afternoon and decided that I would
love you
I love you I love you I love you

Poem

like a will-o'-the-wisp in the night
on a honeysuckle breeze
a moment sticks
us together

like a dolphin being
tickled on her stomach
my sea of love flip-flops all
over my face

like the wind blowing
across a field of wheat
your smile whispers to my inner ear

with the relief of recognition
i bend to your eyes
casually
raping me

Luxury

i suppose living
in a materialistic society
luxury
to some would be having
more than what you need

living in an electronic age seeing
the whole world by pushing a button
the *nth* degree might perhaps be
adequately represented by having
someone there to push
the buttons for you

i have thought if only
i could become rich and famous i would
live luxuriously in new york knowing
famous people eating
in expensive restaurants calling
long distance anytime i want

but you held me
one evening and now i know
the ultimate luxury
of your love

When I Nap

when i nap
usually after 1:30
because the sun comes
in my room then
hitting the northeast
corner

i lay at the foot
of my bed and smell
the sweat of your feet
in my covers
while i dream

The Butterfly

those things
which you so laughingly call
hands are in fact two
brown butterflies fluttering
across the pleasure
they give
my body

I Want To Sing

i want to sing
a piercing note
lazily throwing my legs
across the moon
my voice carrying all the way
over to your pillow
i want you

i need i swear to loll
about the sun
and have it smelt me
the ionosphere carrying
my ashes all
the way over
to your pillow
i want you

Rain

rain is
god's sperm falling
in the receptive
woman how else
to spend
a rainy day
other than with you
seeking sun and stars
and heavenly bodies
how else to spend
a rainy day
other than with you

How Do You Write a Poem?

how do you write a poem
about someone so close
to you that when you say ahhhhh
they say chuuuu
what can they ask you to put
on paper that isn't already written
on your face
and does the paper make it
any more real
that without them
life would be not
impossible but certainly
more difficult
and why would someone need
a poem to say when i come
home if you're not there
i search the air
for your scent
would i search any less
if i told the world
i don't care at all
and love is so complete
that touch or not we blend
to each other the things
that matter aren't all about
baaaanging (i can be baaaanged all
day long) but finding a spot

where i can be free
of all the physical
and emotional bullshit
and simply sit with a cup
of coffee and say to you
"i'm tired" don't you know
those are my love words
and say to you "how was your
day" doesn't that show
i care or say to you "we lost
a friend" and not want to share
that loss with strangers
don't you already know
what i feel and if
you don't maybe
i should check my feelings

Just a New York Poem

i wanted to take
your hand and run with you
together toward
ourselves down the street to your street
i wanted to laugh aloud
and skip the notes past
the marquee advertising "women
in love" past the record
shop with "The Spirit
In The Dark" past the smoke shop
past the park and no
parking today signs
past the people watching me in
my blue velvet and i don't remember
what you wore but only that i didn't want
anything to be wearing you
i wanted to give
myself to the cyclone that is
your arms
and let you in the eye of my hurricane and know
the calm before

and some fall evening
after the cocktails
and the very expensive and very bad
steak served with day-old baked potatoes
after the second cup of coffee taken

while listening to the rejected
violin player
maybe some fall evening
when the taxis have passed you by
and that light sort of rain
that occasionally falls
in new york begins
you'll take a thought
and laugh aloud
the notes carrying all the way over
to me and we'll run again
together
toward each other
yes?

Telephone Poem

Cans and strings and backyard trees
Giggles coming through the wire
Summer mud pies lemonade stands
Hang Up No You Hang Up First

Potatoes must be piled mile high
Then you add the leaves
Daddies always light the fires
Hang Up No You Hang Up First

Marriage children divorce jobs
Ambitions eat our days away
Girl I miss our silly times
Hang Up No You Hang Up First

You Came, Too

I came to the crowd seeking friends
I came to the crowd seeking love
I came to the crowd for understanding

I found you

I came to the crowd to weep
I came to the crowd to laugh

You dried my tears
You shared my happiness

I went from the crowd seeking you
I went from the crowd seeking me
I went from the crowd forever

You came, too

Her Flying Trapeze

Some see the world through rose colored glasses
Some can't see the forest for the trees
A stitch in time will always save nine
She rides through the trees with the greatest of ease
Alone on her flying trapeze

Some will tell you the glass is half full
Others see it as mostly empty
An ounce of prevention is one pound of cure
She flies through the sky two tattoos on her thigh
Alone on her flying trapeze

Some ride the Steinway's 88
Some drive an 18 wheeler
Some feel like fools in their gasoline mules
She glides through the breeze with an absolute ease
Alone on her flying trapeze

I Take Master Card

(Charge Your Love To Me)

I've heard all the stories
'bout how you don't deserve me
'cause I'm so strong and beautiful and wonderful and you could
never live up to what you know I should have but I just want to let
you know:

I take Master Card

You can love me as much as your heart can stand
then put the rest on
account and pay the interest
each month until we get this settled

You see we modern women do comprehend
that we deserve a whole lot more
than what is normally being offered but we are trying
to get aligned with the modern world

So baby you can love me all
you like 'cause you're pre-approved
and you don't have to sign on
the bottom line

Charge it up
'til we just can't take no more
it's the modern way

I take Master Card
to see your Visa
and I deal with a Discovery but I don't want any American
Express 'cause like the Pointer Sisters say: I need a slow hand

In All Seasons

For Clinton on his 80th Birthday Celebration

I have no quarrel . . . with the energy of Spring . . . I rather enjoy
. . . the baying of the winds . . . calling to the new moons . . . I like
the day time heat . . . and the night time cooling . . . when Spring
comes around

As a lover of tomatoes . . . my own homegrown . . . I respect the heat
. . . of a Summer's day . . . I TV. the Atlanta Braves . . . and cheer
my head off . . . for the number one place . . . Yes, Summer is clearly
. . . an important time of year . . . We incubate the Earth . . . to enjoy
its fruits

And Fall . . . Autumn is always welcome by we . . . though I can't
can and don't quilt . . . I polish my old leather boots . . . and air my
blankets . . . I stack my wood . . . and illegally record my winter's
movies from my video rental place . . . I watch the moon and wait

I love the smell . . . of Winter soup simmering . . . all day on the
stove . . . The white caps on the mountain top as I anticipate the
white hair on my head . . . signaling not my physical survival so
much . . . as my emotional commitment . . . to continue the adven-
ture . . . of life . . . in all . . . seasons